Also by Michael Nipert

———————

Reveille

THE FIELD

THE FIELD

by

Michael Nipert

Book and cover design: VertVolta Design

Cover photograph : © Patty Swartzwelder
Tree rings photo: © Joel Jasmin via Unsplash

ISBN: 979-8-9909921-1-5

Published by
Nightbird Press
Michael Nipert, Seattle WA
michaelnipert.com

In honor of my Nana and Grampa
and my Mom and Dad, for their unselfish love,
beautiful passion, and uncommon wisdom.

Contents

The Origin of the Field

The field began in the mind of man, or maybe a divine hand, a place like Eden perhaps, a meadow, a glade of wildflowers and sweet shade on a hot day. The openness was there to fill with a dream, with pastoral peace, or a vision of love enduring with all the little attentions that create the way into the land above, the suspended space where the heart is full of emotion and the soul is the breeze caressing your face. Where the field began, we all began to sense through play through passion through visions of our becoming a trace of heaven.

My Grampa, George Ouimet, imagined horses on an endless plain, chestnuts and bays, their manes blown and fluted as they raced with the wind. He used to ride his pony to school each day, and when he grew bored, he would just disappear into the hills riding toward what he could imagine. He quit school after the fifth grade and began hitchhiking over the Cascade Mountains to the auctions in Yakima where he listened to wild tales and learned the secrets of the horse from the old horse traders.

At fifteen, after his father died from injuries incurred in a coal mine collapse, he worked in the fields in Canada, which were not the field he imagined, in order to support his mother and other members of the family. After a couple years he returned to Washington and married half of his dream, my Nana, Katie Odonin. He proceeded to work in the dark shafts and clotted air of the coal mines in Black Diamond and Newcastle for several years. He was well aware of the danger, but his dream was still visible somewhere up ahead in the haze of the years to come. He could see it in flashes and hear it audible as horse hooves pounding on the drum of his own land and racing with the wind at the track. Chestnuts and bays in the blur as he slaved away through the deep dark tunnels of the mines.

Eventually it all happened, the land, the horses, the glory of racing and winning at the track. Waking up to his cleanly fenced ranch, the oats and hay, the water he would carry in buckets to his brood, the connection to every inch of his land with the gyp-ring and pathways he made with his tractor. The big barns stuffed with yellow straw and the redolent green of timothy and alfalfa, the tac room filled with bridles, halters and leather saddles, the color and scent of it all so strong in my memory. This was the world where I was raised inside his dream, the field he made where I woke to my dreams of innocent connection to the animals and the imagined world of Never Never Land, the magic of the game of baseball and the perception of the infinite from the field expanding.

Seeing the Field

Shaping the Field

Every morning wiping
a summery sleep from
my eyes and looking out
over Grampa's work: the field
drug flat in the upper corner,
a gyp-ring with the tractor,
ten acres of fences defining
the separate spaces, apple trees,
cherries and plum, my Grampa
carrying buckets of water.

He talks to his wild yet
behaved horses in modulations
they seem to understand.

He gives Connie Rose a slap
on the flanks; she bursts
into a gallop that the rest
of the chestnuts follow,
like a hive of big orange bees.

Rainy Day Blur

Board games, building models,
in the dry basement with
the neighborhood crew,
slip away from the others
and out into the weather,
a soaking ceaseless enough
to drive the horses under
the big umbrella trees.

The snorts and steam rising
from their slippery backs,
beneath the plywood nailed
to the low hanging branches,
where I lay whispering their
names and reaching down
to stroke their damp manes.

After some imagining
and much hesitation,
once again slip out,
this time from under
my slick skin and slide
onto the back of No Friction.

He busts out through the branches,
bareback apparition strutting
through the dreaded drench

with me around the field
holding tight against his neck,
whispering soft chants,
my beaded words circling
the soft shapes of the coral
through the rainy-day blur.

Letting My Eyes Out

I don't know when it started,
when it became a Jedi trick
of the spirit and perception,
but I have very early memories
of being poised in a tree,
looking off the deck
in the early morning mist,
or standing at the fence
calling out for the horses
and letting my eyes out.

Later, the transcendent would come
from this homespun Renton meditation,
but these early sensations of freedom
are some of my most precious to recall.

When I feel I have fallen
into the noise and shattering
indifference of the middle world,
with all its prisoners of puppetry
in a reflected and reflecting reality,
I let my eyes out again
and fill the space of my seeing
with a tingling presence
as I had when I was young
when the whole field of perception
pulsed within the borders of my body.

The horses pounding through the field,
the reformulation of the hanging mist,
the dream of Never Never Land
calling from the distance, all became
the body of my imagination.

The muscular force of the horses,
a sharp nip on the arm,
the sweet juice of the blackberry
and the prick of its thorn,
these are all palpable portents
of the real but they do not
explain or eclipse the expanding
sense of the field on another plane.
What begins with the physical
may rise with an inverse gravity
when the eyes are let out and
the vertiginous light of the spirit unites.

Even the animals, our dog Shadow,
the sleek chestnut Blondie Spin,
would on occasion respond to this sensation.
I imagined more sentient souls,
like Saint Francis of Assisi,
and let my eyes out in the field.

The Torch of the Horse

Inside me still the horses
arch their necks, snort, strut,
and thunder through the field.

They are lathered with sweat.
They beat the drum of my heart
with a percussion of hooves.
They are still wild in the wind
with their chestnut manes
tossing from side to side.

I see them galloping together
across the expansive hillside.
No bit, no reins, no fence
binds them in their minds.
Theirs is a passion
for speed and power.

They bust through the cobwebs
of culture, the petty preoccupation
with submission; they trample
this weakness within me.

Half horse, half man, my Grampa
taught me to be like them.
The horse mixed his blood
with a passion to be free

on that lush open range,
a torch in hand riding above
the prescriptions of the town.

Nature found a tremendous force
when it slipped into the horse
and broke its yoke open on the wind.

Inside me still the horses
arch their necks, snort, strut
and thunder through the field.

What Rises from Play

Because no one would kill the chickens
my Grampa decided we are no longer a farm
and made a ranch instead to raise
and train his thoroughbreds.

When they returned from the track
in late August each year,
they would gallop from end to end
of the field and nicker and neigh.
They loved those grass munching days.

Alongside the thrum of hooves,
the ecstatic games we played:
climbing high in the trees
swinging to the rhythm of the wind,
games of meadow and woods-run,
pinecone wars and catching snakes,
or on our backs in the high grass
staring into the stars
at the worlds beyond.

I was grown in this field
like a stalk of corn or a sunflower,
fed by the force of the horses,
determined like my Grampa's chin.

I felt the invisible presence
with my Nana since I was young.

The winds ran their fingers
through the tall grasses;
my spirit rose through the porous sky.
I ran wild through the field
and afar for freedom.

Rooted here, watered, loved and known,
I was called by the unknown
deeper into nature and beyond.

The surprise of rising above
the body, above the face
of the sunflower reflecting sun.

Why we are chosen to this
and what circumstances hatch
the soul into many places at once
remains a part of the mystery.

We are more than flesh and bone.
Even some of the animals know
what those on the busy road
have long ago forgotten.

Beauty and the Field

The intergalactic kaleidoscope,
the placenta of the new-born child,
beauty organizes out of itself,
daisies and marigolds,
the careening tilt of a hawk's flight,
the sight and scent of our
enchantment beyond expedience.

With all that has happened here
both in the past and recent years
we have had to sell the inexplicable
beauty that has flourished in the field.

The future construction features
some twenty or more luxury homes.
They say there will still be at least
forty fir trees along the back fence line,
and that they're going to name it
Bridle Trails Enclave, in honor
of the horse ranch that thrived here,

but what I see is that the fecundity
of the field, with its great ant hills
and apple trees, with its patches
of wildflowers and abundant berries,
with all that slithers and scuttles through

the scotch broom and thatched weeds,
will soon be bulldozed under a deep sleep.

What is left of the pulse and spirit
of this place will come up only
through the ornamental cracks
of a predictable symmetry,
but the lesson of the field
for us who carry the memory
will not be lost - for the field exists
perpetually on the endless plane.

In the space between
unkempt nature and knowing,
imagination is born out of itself,
runs like the child with abandon,
each act of play a step closer.

He climbs up into the trees,
follows the trajectory of the rainbow.
Oh, do not let it go!
We were born to grow
from this staggering beauty.

Family Picnics

The field was a symbol of unity
and the fences, the arms and
clutched hands of our family.

When I was younger, the big picnics
always took place at Nana and Grampa's.
Everyone in Dick and Ann's family
and ours would be there within
the circle that held it all together.

We played croquet in the mown grass
of the big front yard: the Easter egg
colors of the balls I'd send far
from the wickets, the echoing laughter,
my uncle Dick and brother Rick
promising to return the favor.
Although I never played that game
beyond those family gatherings,
I would wake up imagining a win
and bounce around Grampa's boots
as he set up the course.

At dinner, I remember Dick always
sneaking back for more gnocchi,
Nana's amazing recipe,
brought over from old Italy.
I gorged on the ravioli.

The wise eyes of Nana smiling,
the electricity of my Mom and Grampa,
the story telling and crescendos of laughter.

Kathy and Karen were like sisters back then.
The gentle voice of Dick as he attended
to the little things still reverberates in my memory.
He always swept up the tables and did the dishes,
as we ran into the fields with our cousins
to pet the horses and share our haunts and hideouts.
The little kids, as we called them, would trail
behind us, Pat with the fire of his Irish red hair
inherited from Grampa, Jeff already with
the composed demeanor of his father
and, looking back, Kim, who was even then
carrying that unique intuition that passed
down through the women in our family.

Sometimes Mary and Terry would come, one
of Nana's sisters and her son.
Other layers of the family would also show up
with cake and ice cream or a late bottle of wine.
Everyone together; it could not last forever.

The Early Years

When Grampa was alive,
the fences were always sturdy
and taut as a tight rope.

When a board began to rot
or was cracked by a horse hoof
or chewed by some muscular jaw,
he replaced it with fresh wood.

Even the wild grasses in the field
were cropped low by the happy brood.

When my Grampa was alive,
this little ranch was under control,
no proliferation of the scotch broom.

The clusters of fir tree were thinned
to keep the open pasture
for the horses to gallop and graze.

Through my early years,
my imagination began to grow
in this nurturing light.
It started with wild horses
leaping the fences like deer.

I would be on one of their backs
and we would bound endless through
the hills where the sun spun round
the world with a light-yellow yarn.

In the last month before he died
of cancer, my Grampa rode around
on a little tractor with an oxygen tank
trying to keep the place as kempt

as he remembered but it had already
begun to fade from the clear distinctions
of what he thought was right.

Big Tree

Counting rings on the Big Tree,
the inside story of the mystery,
considering that it is now 2015,
I finger my way to when I was born,
the year I climbed near the top,
the year I rode out the storm,
high in the branches, taking chances
to feel the sap and pulse within.

There is more to this than my memory,
over a hundred years in the wind,
the roots that had spread wide and deep
in the tall solitude of a standing vigil
to keep a stoic view of each
niche and corner of the field:
the hawks that settled in the branches,
the horses galloping poetry below,
the children imagining the advances
of enemy armies in the snow.

To know the perspective of growing
old this rooted to the same view,
like my Nana looking from her window
at the flood of Scotch Broom in the field,

this tree had one great purpose
to spread wide its green wings
beneath the light of golden glances
in the trance of its own being.

Maternal Magic

Her Fading Eyes

She waited in the faded white
house at ninety for each day
to peel away one more desire
The fences in the field
that for so many years
held the world inside
had begun to rot

The scotch broom and groves
of fir had invaded
the openness her man
had cleared and kept
for the horses
to thunder and feed –
the old gray barn that stored
the saddle, tacking, and hay
collapsing like a lung
dangerous beyond repair

These things did not hurt her
They were no longer her concern

She had come to the window
where she could watch the children
turn up from the past
with their games in the dark

with their hands in the
hands of their children
holding the chain unbroken
flawless to her fading eyes

Cards, Cookies, and Milk

Whenever the confusion of youth rattled too hard, or my mother made my head whirl with her wild emotions, I would walk 384 feet down the field, hop the fence, and walk inside the hearth to see my Nana. From the moment you entered the old white house, there was the smell of horse hair and my Grampa's famous iodine anodyne for taking the swelling out of the ankles and knees of his thoroughbreds. Garlic and an array of spices also hung lightly in the air, as you sat at the kitchen table and joined my Nana looking out the window at the ten-acre expanse. The strongest scent, however, was the indescribable fragrance of my Nana, a light mint in a musky smoke, medicinal as well. You could never write it down, like my Grampa's secret recipe for inflammation which he whispered to one man only before he died.

My Nana would always pour a glass of milk for me and bring out the oatmeal cookies with peanuts inside. Dipping the cookie in the milk, I would watch her shuffle a deck of cards and deal them out for a new game to learn. She was the one who taught me how to pick up a splay of cards and in one deft movement, shuffle and deal. In addition to the new games, she taught me how to feel my way through the hands I had been dealt. I would tell her why I was so upset, the lack of loyalty in friends, the foolishness of coaches or teachers, the unfairness of it all. She would chuckle lightly and say little, but she knew; she understood. Between the hands we played, she would praise me for my strengths, and her scent would stir around the room, like cream in a cup of coffee. By the time I would leave, every time, my thoughts would be clear, my heart strong, and that scent would walk with me out the door like a kind of knowing I would make my own.

When I later decided to leave my PhD program in Santa Barbara to transfer to the University of Washington, a major impetus was to move my children back so they could grow up close to our aging Nana. She had come from a line of strong and mysterious women. Her mother, Noni, had been a deeply spiritual woman and a healer as well before she moved to New Orleans from Turin, Italy, where people had come from neighboring towns for her subtle medicines.

As my mother remembers: when the family had moved to Orelia, after Cle Elum, to the western side of the Cascade Mountains, Noni would feed the wandering vagrants looking for work and a hot meal. It was the late thirties and still the Depression, and she made large pots of soup to feed whoever was in need. My mother told me all throughout my childhood that Noni was the most beautiful, most spiritual woman she ever knew. The animals and birds would gather around her without fear. Noni's mother had also been a healer and her mother from further south in Calabria, but all I really know is that Nana had an invisible touch and presence. She was the one who brought me to the healing waters.

My children understood quickly what I told them about my Nana, and she became their Nana too. When Byron, my oldest son, reached the stage of adolescent turmoil, he would ask me to take him to Nana, and whatever passed between them, he walked away again and again feeling and believing in a better way.

The day before my Nana died at 96, she rallied herself up out of the confusion of the drugs they were giving her for the immense pain of the cancer and MRSA that had riddled her body. She was lucid and wise as she had always been, as she told each of us something beautiful before she parted. She told me that I had always been her star and that she knew I was going to take good care of those boys of mine.

Although she died the next day and many years have passed, she has never been far from our thoughts. I even moved into her old white house for a couple of years, to save money and be closer to her I imagine. The cupboards and counters and coffee tables were covered with pictures of her children, grandchildren, and great grandchildren. My nieces would ask me if her ghost ever came to me, or if I would see her in my dreams. I played a lot of cards at the kitchen table. I drank from her favorite cups and ate off her dishes. The scent of her alongside my childhood was everywhere. It is with me now as I write down these memories. May she never pass away.

Ancient Knowing

When my mom was young, only a few people lived on this old road. Everything behind them was forest and field peppered with random houses, right up into the foothills of the Cascades. The open space, peoples' place in nature, was an everyday reminder of sun and moon, of the ministry of morning songbirds, of the ominous presence of the bear, of the elegant grace of the deer, of the irrepressible hunger that drives all living animals thrashing through the green world of flesh.

So much change in less than a century, the once gravel road now constantly congested with the phlegm of cars and trucks and the incessant white noise hissing like a snake, until the screech of brakes escalate the intrusion and everything comes to a stop. The new homes are lined up in rows and even the people are somehow not the same, formed by a regularity, deaf within their clamor, blind within their artificial light. Not that the people who came before simply knew more,

or were without struggle and frustration, but many, like my Nana, or Noni, or my Mom, knew how to listen to the voice in silence, to the soul of the animals, to the suggestions of the splendor of light. To some, everything in nature presented an argument for what was beyond. This was not spilled religion, but rather an ancient knowing that comes from attention and living in the rhythm that rolls a river through the leaves. In this ten acre field where I was raised to full height, I heard drumbeats of hooves and the voices of night and wind and star and felt some presence larger than myself pulling me out into the endless expanse – blue sky above the open field – into spirit.

My Mother's Nature

My Mother was raised here and left for seven years at most.
A little like Rappaccini's daughter in Hawthorne's tale,
her beauty and sense of nature are inextricable from this land.
Selling all but her house and less than an acre,
there will be little left for her to let her eyes out,
or for the animals to come like spirits blessed to her doorstep.

Dogs, cats, birds, deer, raccoon, even a duck,
the animals have come to her with uncanny trust.
Even the horses, loyal to my Grampa like devoted soldiers,
loved her the best: Alibhai, the champion, would strut
across the field when he saw her in the backyard,
bow his neck, snort, and blow out his lips
for her to come and give him affection.

She has watered and fed both the wild and domesticated.
She has always said that the animals, even the mice and squirrels,
are closer to God, not because of something she's read,
but rather because she feels it as the force of beauty
that presses through the green world in so many forms.

Of course, she went to school like the others,
but the field was her classroom and teacher.
It was her ark where she kept creation alive
amid the flood of corruption on the outside.

It taught her a kind of knowing that has always astonished me.
Give her a scrap of a person's character and she can tell you
quickly who they are and what they are about.
What the Taoists call direct intuition is strong in her,
the deep understanding that precedes the word,
sometimes even the senses; praise to the field wherever
you find it, in Wordsworth's England, or even here in Renton.

Past Present

She slips in and out of the present
like a thread trying to sew
the past back into her head

On horseback long black hair
on her back and shoulders
streaming at a gallop through the air,

her pursed lips whistle and chirp
to go a little faster within the border
of the fences around the field.
The centrifugal force of adventure
takes her further up through

the trails and old logging roads
into the foothills of the mountains.
This freedom, bred from a love of above
and her horse, Princess Littlebit,
lithely strides up into the passes
where she slips through the eye
of the needle for a moment,
as she sits in her chair now eighty,
well beyond the riding stages.

The freedom then after chores,
on days when there was no school,

to ride solitary or with her brother
and friends into the world her God intended.
It can be so painful to reach back,
her mother, father and husband dead.
The many names of animals withered,
without their stories being told,
also take away her breath when memory
seizes their absence; even the hills
she had known have grown
infested with suburban sprawl,

and now she frets late into the night
as the traffic thins on the boisterous road.
She has had to sell the sacred field
from the burden of bloated taxes.

She counts again the various places
where the dogs have been buried
and prays for the sanctity of their bones.

She hears her mother and father's voices;
she prays they can abide by what she has done.

Even if they could give her their blessing,
slip through and consecrate the present
choices she and her brother have made,
even if they knew the city had expanded

and the field was surrounded by hundreds
of fluorescent houses and menaced all day
and night by the cacophonous traffic,
there is no reconciliation for endless loss,
a battle of continual failure, the collapse
of the body, like the barns and fences,
the memories plowed under by bulldozers,
the crunching teeth and gurgling noises
of a big beast devouring the deepest
and dearest of her memories…

but for the present, the grandchildren,
great grandchildren and the wisdom
from Noni and Nana, George and John
and on and on through the needle
into the present, the goodness
of Saint Francis, the unspeakable beauty
of nature and all its creatures, love
and how it hurts and how it has grown.
She cannot, will not let them down.
The past into the present and the deepest
kind of knowing that can and cannot be spoken
beckon her to carry on the love that is gone.

Mother

She brought God down close to earth.
"The animals are better than people," she said,
and the animals knew she meant it.
The birds heard the word and clustered
in her trees as the raccoon and deer nestled near.

She would stay awake through the darkest
nights to talk us through our loss of sight.
A hand, a ride, something deep inside
drove her to deliver us and more,
the other children who came to her door.

She raised us to believe in the first light,
that the sun itself was the gift of life,
that flowers and trees, shrubs and weeds
were all the children of his delight.
His presence knelt beside her in church;
she brought God down close to earth.

As children we thought she might be a witch.
What is bad, who to trust, what we did
in the dark of night out of sight,
we thought she simply knew too much.

Unselfish acts through sacrifice,
a condition she knew so well,
she would bring the spirit within reach
to catch each child before they fell.

Now the loss of her from our world
is a gaping hole we must fill.
She has gone back to earth
and beyond the wind with her will.
By her example we must learn
to give more than we take

and heed the word she must have heard
that brought God down so close
our souls began to wake.

Further Afield

Dreamscape

The field is a dreamscape,
sunlight and manna dew.
We used to climb to the top
of the big tree and sway
with the breezes, look out
over the treetops and imagine
a land of endless wilderness.

We called it Never Never Land,
a land that never ceased.
This must have been a feeling
that drove early settlers
feeling small as children
seeking further and further west.

We imagined flying saucers
and when we explored the unknown land,
the flying saucers came with heavy
shadows and high-pitched sounds
that drove the dog to flopping his ears.
We dropped the shovels and hammers
we brought to make a fort
and scattered like bees.

One day while alone in the field,
I found the end of a rainbow

and although there was no pot
of gold, my body turned
vertiginous in that light.

Playing hide and seek,
I tried to see through objects,
and I came to know
when the enemy was near
through a slight pulsation of sense,
the same way the horses
knew our fear.

After school and sports
crammed my brain with transitive
figures and mundane repetition,
I would return to my neighborhood
and the field that grew with each
adventure deeper into the unknown.
There was no lid on the imagination
once we were home.

Trek to Never Never Land

We never talked about it much
when we came back together.

Strange and unexpected,
a shrill sound intensified

above us, as the light
turned metallic and cold.

It's a spaceship, Steve shouted,
and we scattered like sparks.

I know nothing else but the colors
that bled through the forest in flight.

I found myself alone, out of breath,
and convinced such things existed.

My little brother, Pat,
would later camp out alone

on the flat in the field with his
space helmet and instrumentation

believing that the UFO's
were bound to return.

We never talked about it much
but I still wonder what they imagined

out beyond the fences
amongst tremulous shadows

before we returned to see
everything strikingly normal.

Pat and the Magic Hats

As children, imagination was the crop we grew out in the field. The Mad Captain with his unending array of games and the endless adventures we dreamed up in the apple trees. From green to red we fed on that fruit like it was ambrosia for our dreams all throughout the freedom of summer. Hanging out in the branches, we made up new words and phrases that we thought might catch fire and spread throughout our schools and told each other stories of what would happen on our next excursion. The big kids, as we called ourselves, ventured further and further afield to find the next mystery, and the Mad Captain would often tell the younger kids wild tales of our discoveries.

When my little brother Pat was young, he exhibited great curiosity and was drawn to adventure as well. He also had a penchant for unusual hats, and our dad slowly brought him an impressive collection that he kept in a big box in the closet, from which he selected his imagined character for each day. When he became obsessed with Charlie Brown and the aerial battles between Snoopy and the Red Baron, our dad built him a Sopwith Camel, a wooden two-winged biplane that you could pull around the yard with a rope. Pat spent many hours out there in the cockpit wearing his vintage aviator hat. His imagination flourished as he constantly drew pictures of his various characters and adventures. He loved to draw and later became a musician and a poet; imagination seized his mind from an early age.

I will always remember that time after our great trek to Never Never Land where a UFO seemed to descend upon us. Pat became obsessed with the existence of these extra-terrestrial entities and began collecting a hodge podge of instrumentation, and of course our father found him a great space helmet. Although he was quite young, around ten I think, he started sleeping out by himself up on the flats in the field, certain that a UFO would come find him and open up communication. My mother and I would worry about him out there by himself all night, although the danger, other than the horses, who were tucked away in the in the barns, was negligible. She would have me sneak up and check on him without him knowing I was there. I would peak through the branches of the young fir trees that had grown around the indented circle that had once been a well but had been filled up with dirt. Over time, however, it had become a little sunken spot as if there was a force underground pulling it down. I was always a little leery of it, imagining while you were standing there that it might just drop into the abyss.

I would see Pat on the flats with his little lights flashing from his space gear, fast at work with his telescope, diligently waiting for the UFO's to descend again and reveal themselves to him. He was adamant in his belief in them and gave us his reports each morning. I don't remember exactly what he saw out there, but I believe he recorded it somewhere. When I was younger, I imagined I was from Mars, or somewhere beyond this planet, and had latent telepathic and clairvoyant abilities. Growing up in the field the way we did, it was no wonder that I had such creative friends and such a brother as Pat.

Escape

Hide and seek in the field –
one person "it," nine others scrambling,
eyes closed for a twenty second count,
loud enough to carry through the wind –
The Little Trees, the upper left corner
of alder and blackberry, the woodpile
beyond the flats, the Big Tree, up
in the Moosermo fort, or climbing
a random fir, everyone dispersing
within the five acres of the biggest field –

The search starting slowly, a sighting,
catch and touch a few of the slower kids
and begin to spread "it" like a contagion.
The bursts of laughter echoing rapid footsteps,
the rush of an occasional horse breaking
from grazing in the grass to a gallop.

The last ones left, climbing into the fir trees,
pursued by several contagious climbers until
they are trapped and forced to acquiesce,
or slide down the outside of the branches,
holding on like a desperate hug, hitting
the ground running and running,
from the inevitable capture.

The Mad Captain

1. IMAGINATION

We called him the Mad Captain because he lit the torch beneath our adventures and games. He got his title on one of our excursions down the Cedar River on a big yellow raft. He stood at the prow brandishing a stick like a sword as we rode into the dangerous rapids about to crash into a log jam. He was the only one who couldn't swim, and Rick shouted, "Our captain is crazy. He's the Mad Captain." Every week or two Steve concocted something new or brought back old favorites with a fresh design. He had a wild imagination, and our creations and adventures were endless. Forts, planes, chemistry set bombs, and excursions into the mountains on the box cars of trains, the sense of play was insatiable. I remember everyone zipping themselves up in the bottoms of sleeping bags and developing strategies to bowl over the armless and eyeless enemy out in the apple field.

Steve and my brother Rick created elaborate World War II naval battles, carefully cutting the proportions of ships out of thick cardboard and working out dice roll ratios for their speed and the size of their guns: destroyers, cruisers, battleships and aircraft carriers. They used historical sites and fought the battles again with different strategies. The Bismarck, the Missouri, the Yamamoto, they had every major ship recorded in play. Later they built models of each ship they could find in stores or magazines. When they completed the formidable fleets, we took them down to the pond in the lower field and floated them out from opposing sides to sink each other's ships with BB guns from the hillside. The games were too many to recount. Every day the imagination lit the field with play.

The Mad Captain also led us on explorations into every neighborhood we could find on bike or on foot. We went into the hills, all day excursions into Squaw, Cougar and Tiger mountains. All day rides into surrounding towns and cities, the field kept expanding. Much of what we did was just childhood exuberance and the growth of imagination, although mischief grew with greater frequency as adolescence led us into a number of questionable situations. On the weekends we started going down to Camp Freeman, where the Boy Scouts came to camp on the hillside just above the Cedar River. At first, we just threw rocks from the dark into their fires or stealthily plucked the pegs from their tents when they were zipped up for the night. Shadow, our gregarious black lab, would come wagging his heavy tail around their campfire angling for food. They would get excited that there was a friendly dog in the middle of the woods, and they would pet and feed him. The Boy Scouts should have suspected that he was a kind of foreshadowing of what was yet to come.

2. Mischief

One Saturday night, we decided to hike a mile down the switchbacks to snoop around on the flat ground next to the river. We had been there before and had found the big supply tents full of camping gear. What we didn't know is that Steve had told some older kids about it, and they had come and stolen as much as they could carry. As we were walking across an open field, suddenly the ranger, who we called Ranger Rick, came barreling toward us. "Stop where you are," he yelled, as the Mad Captain raised his walking stick like a rifle and sharply shouted "bang!" The older looking man dropped like a rock to the ground. I started to approach concerned about a heart attack, when half lifting himself from the dirt, he yelled loudly to the barracks: "they are back!" Larger than life eagle scouts came bounding out in numbers. "Run," Steve cried, and run we did. Straight up the steep banks, anxiously looking back at the closing distance between us and them. They had one of those "go everywhere, do anything machines" and flashlights in their hands. They looked like robots marching faster the steeper it got. I felt this sudden shot of nitro in my blood, and I left everyone in the dust.

I was breathless and alone when I reached the top, except for my shadow, my dog Shadow, who I barely lifted over the six-foot fence, then turned around to look for Rick, Steve, and Skip. It seemed like five minutes before Steve and Skip shambled toward me, yelling "run! They're on our heels and they got a jeep." I bounded the fence and Steve and Skip climbed over it behind me. We sprinted into the Briarwood South neighborhood at full speed, as the jeep whined down the streets looking for us. Running through backyards, chased by dogs, porch lights splashing at our feet, people shouting from their stoops, we made our way toward Never Never Land. The young men in the jeep caught a last glimpse of us as we waved to them and disappeared into the dark entrance of the 75 acres of woods. When we had clearly lost them, we came to our senses like waking up from a dream. "Where is Rick," I exclaimed? Steve said, "we have to go back and find him. We lost him somewhere on the hill."

After about a mile back toward trouble, there was Rick, my brother, jaunting along, arms swinging high, and whistling a tune. "What happened to you," we all cried out. He said, "I fell about half-way up. They were getting close, so I laid low in the bushes. They stomped right past my head. Their boots were huge; they must have been giants. I just waited for them to be gone. I knew they'd take the switchbacks on the way down." We all had a good laugh and headed for home. That was the last time we haunted Camp Freeman.

Snow Play

When the snow invaded
with soft petals drifting
from the plentitude above,
an endless onslaught of quiet
came with memories of sled runs
and rolling up snowmen
with button eyes
and ice-cream complexions,
carrot noses and smokeless pipes,

when the children shouted
and stuck out their tongues,
flake after flake, a kind of communion,
and the commotion grew
with snowballs and ice forts,
and exuberance knew no bounds.

We stepped out of our years
from the window watching
our snow angels forming
on the white pristine page;

we awoke from deep slumber
with the light pouring out
from the mystery above
the secret of play.

Caravan of Bees

That afternoon when the wind
blew so balmy and heavy you could
lean into its arms as it held you
from falling to the ground

my brother and I began laughing
as we ran around in circles and found
ourselves grown dizzy in the anomaly

This was when a warm swarm of bees
blew through on that strange wind
and circled the yard in a blur of color
and musical murmuring sounds

until they seemed to land at once
on a low bough of a backyard tree
a humming trance of a big ball of bees

With urgency our mother called to my
brother and me to get in the house
She told us it was dangerous out there
with that great swarm ten times
the size of any hive I had ever seen

We watched from the window for days
as the scouts flew out and buzzed
around the yard to guard the queen

while others searched further afield
for a place to build their combs of honey

Those days were magical for me
that concentrated force and hum
that meditational om of the bees

that were delivered on a tropical carpet
to our house where they grew so calm
and quiet that they entered into me
standing for hours at the window
or lying in my bed attentively listening

I wondered at their presence and longed
for them to stay before the beekeeper came

and swept them into a big black case
to place them closer to where that tropical
wind whisked them away like Ariel and her
fairies on a long and enchanting journey

Cedar River

Those early explorations took us deeper and
deeper into nature, up in the nearby mountains
and down the rapids of the Cedar River.

We would try to brave it early each year
with the spring melt high on the banks.

The first plunge would take your breath away,
the gasping and thrashing to stay above water.

Late April, early May, tubing the bends and
twists and the log jams that altered every year.
Dread surprise around the corner of the rapids.

The thrill of bouncing through the rushes,
so turbulent you sometimes lost your tube,

hands helping each other stay afloat
through the inescapable snarl and log jam.

Learning when to step back and get out of the water.
Sometimes hours of floating and slow spinning
through a canopy of green and flickering light,

fish beneath winnowing through the currents;
stories told, stories unfolding, floating toward
another time, tell-tale signs, Rhonda Lee

on a rope swing, couldn't get her svelte body,
the curve of her hips, out of my mind.

The near drownings, the exhilarating rapids,
the glide through shadow and light, the slow
drifting into a new age of the body and the journey.

We would come out at the mouth and kick
across the lake to Coulon Beach; Jennifer Albright
buxom in a halter top. The world was changing.

Orange Dawn

The Salmon swam upriver
to spawn somewhere beyond
where I stood on the rocky shore
stunned by their progress together

They were a sacred gathering
about fifty feet in tow and fifty wide
Orange as if they had been soaked
in an orange dye of sunshine

They spanned the width of the river
as they slipped and shimmied
their way against the current

There would be rapids up ahead
and beaver dams and log jams
before they would make it back
to where they had hatched

I can still see that orange mass
slithering and shimmering upstream
I imagined and still imagine diving
into the middle of them and down

until I reached the luminous
light of the sun shining up from
the bottom like a Chinese lantern

A kind of baptism was offered
in synchronicity with the salmon
dream of a golden place upriver
where their young would be born

year after year to swim their own
way down through silver until they
find the orange dawn together
and forever becomes their song

Paternal Passing

Vantage at Fifty

At fifty my father who I can
never remember ever sick
was struck one fall over in Vantage
by the bell of a stroke.
He had driven over the mountains
to hunt pheasant but could not remember
why he came and for a while
lost even his own name.

He must have stood there and stared
at the sparseness of stubble and tumbleweed,
watched the sluggish river pulse
in the white sheen of the short
sleeved early autumn heat.

Nearly stripped clean in that painful
but vibrant ring he would not
have remembered his three sons
reaching out for him for strength and direction.

He would not have remembered that woman
he loved for her caravan of colors
and fetching feeling.

I wonder if he stood there
about to fall into a deep hole
like the old and empty well

that stands off limits
in the lower field of our farm.

I wonder if he felt the despair
that I feel now at nearly fifty
and unable to hold the world together
for my three sons with the sticks
and stones of unsticking glue.

And I wonder what brought him
back to home and consciousness
to fight through six months

of a malignant brain tumor.
Maybe it was Noah, the black retriever,
with a couple of barks and a sloppy tongue.
I imagine he slowly remembered—

each thought like another bead
on a rosary—that there was more to do,
words he still had to say
to me and both of my brothers
and our poor mother to help us
make it through his passing away.

A Father's Concern

"Those kids gave her a hard time,"
he said, "but she was all sugar
or all shit; she deserved some of it.
She loves them though,
and they're a pretty good bunch."

"Yes," I said, a little staggered,
pounding in a steel post
online with the others, as we
worked together to build a fence.

"Now Ricky has settled down
with Lori and the kids.
He's stopped racing cars
and goes to work every day.
He's beginning to find his place."

I looked at the pleasure on his face.
His eyes took his smile
far away from me.

"Pat's at home still. He'll take care
of his mother when I'm gone.
She'll need him, and he's
dependable as stone."

The shadows from the house,
the wind in my sleeve,
everything felt a little awkward
as I watched his features
grow gray and heavy.

I studied the scar on his head
from the surgery, his hair almost gone
from the radiation, and the tumor
still thriving. "Now Mike," he said
and I could see his eyes begin
to water, and my lips quivered.
His speech began to stammer.
He was not speaking to me.
I must have become some kind
of stranger who he could

show his fears, something
I never suspected as a child.
He would chase away the witches
and demons from my sleep.

"Now Mike," he said, "I'm worried.
After his fall, after his injury in baseball,
he's been lost; he doesn't know
who he is anymore.

I think he's taking drugs.
He's my one concern."

I found myself crawling up
from a dark cave
trying to reach his pain.
He waited for me
to speak or nod my head
but everything suddenly turned rigid.
I could not move to save my life.
"Let's put up the fence," he said.

Later, he was talking to me again.
My father, his son, building a fence
for my mother — to protect
her garden from the dogs.

We spent the rest of the day
together, our last real talk,
just a month before he died.

My Brother's Dream

When my father fell into the bottomless well,
past sight and sound, past touch and smell,
the taste of life probably lingered a little,
but he must have eventually just let go.

I was in Minnesota under a crazy night
of fireflies and endless mosquitoes.
The whole sky would turn white
with sheet lightning. I stayed up
most of the evening just watching.

In the morning I woke up to the news.
"It's your father,' Esther said, and hugged me
long and hard. At first, I thought I was above it,
riding the airplane through the turbulence
all the way back to gray Seattle, but it left a far
deeper hole in me than I was ready to admit.

The next morning my brother Rick told me
of his dream. From what I recall, our Dad
was driving his sons into the mountains,
telling us the things we had to remember
along the way, "you need to take care
of your mother and stay off the drugs."
When we had gone past pavement
up into the flowering meadows,
as far up as his truck would go,

he said, "you need to get out now"
and sent the three of us out on foot.
We began climbing the jagged stone
face of a rock wall when Rick
started calling out, "it's too steep,
I can't do it," then each of us heard it:
"You can make it Ricky; don't give up."
"You can make it," he said, and together
we continued scaling the steep rock
face of the mystery. This was what
Rick heard from him as he woke up.

My Father's Return

We all left the field.
Steve threw an unrolled sleeping bag
over his shoulder and hitchhiked
out of our lives.

Fred I remember
grew too old or too cool
to live in our imagined world
of pinecone tag and climbing trees.

When my father died,
his absence grew so wide
that only his footprints remained,
the house he helped build, the big black
backstop and the steel trailer he welded
together, too large and heavy
to drag off the farm.

I could never reconcile his passing
until he started returning
with his favorite Labrador retriever.
They strode through the tall grass together
bringing home a fullness that sounded
like returning horns from the hunt
and a light that altered in the optic
play of what stood ahead
and what had passed away.

Although these were only dreams,
I understood the nature of return
and the enduring presence of all
the imagination has seized as its own.

The field I said must be a dream
where all the possibilities still remain.

The Returning Dead

How we imagine the dead returning
to life, just as they were. My Grampa,
the Prince of Poverty Row, with a bounce
in his boots, throwing punches in the air,
master of his horses, follow him anywhere.
We see him like Hercules, throwing hay bales,
with the smell of horses and his famous
liniment that took all the pain away
but changed the color of your skin.

I imagine him from what I've missed,
the way he charged the air like lightning,
and Nana with her wisdom deeper
than the deep dug well out back,
with a scent that was like a spell
of an old world healer. You would tell
her all of your troubles and her smile
would make it small and you would
know the power of soul in this world.

My father always came back
through the high grass of the field,
through shades of yellow and violet
with his favorite dog at his feet,
with that unending kindness in his eyes,
making sure none of us were lost,
that none were falling behind.

I had this repeating dream
several times across the years.
He would come back silent and strong
to chase the demons from our sleep.

In our house we share these memories,
tell the stories, each with a different
slant, as everyone listens for the secret.
I swear there is more than memory here,
more than the imagined presence.
The love returns; the love is in the air.

Father

I walk and I feel my father's
steps his dust in my dust

I talk and I hear my father's
voice his timbre in my tone

I know that I am never alone
and when I'm dead I won't be gone

Is it blood to blood that carries
us along or do we belong

to something more than dust to dust
I sing my song for more than me alone

To what is it that we belong
the spirit of man and the great throng

or is it the dirt of the earth
or the salt of the seas and oceans

My mind travels the galaxies beyond
the windows and mirrors of every sun

to each and every one I meet
the steps of my father in my own feet

the love of my brother in our defeat
the voice of the enemy in my own song

and the universe to which we belong
and the spirit that leads to the father beyond

The Loss of Place

Nature Taking Over

When I lived there again,
caretaking the old white house
for several years, long after
my Grampa's death, just a year
after my Nana passed away,

the field had grown thick
with patches of scotch broom and blackberry.
The wild grass no longer cropped low
still made room for bright clusters
of buttercup and daisies.

The stout moss-covered barns sagged
toward the big collapse that came
one year later in the heavy snow.
The deer had made this place their haven.
A family bedded in the Little Trees,
out in the middle of the big field.

As I sat in the backyard
that looked out over the ten acres,
hundreds of songbirds zipped
in and out of the bushes
with a stunning medley of music.

At dusk a big barn owl would land
on a high post and peruse the field

while all day two hawks would glide
between three trees, harried constantly
by brigades of menacing crow.
Nest robbers and dive bombers, the hawks
ruled over the smaller game in the field.

Besides the family of deer who would
come near the house for water
I placed in buckets for them,
there were also families of raccoon
that would traverse the yard

and shred the night with war cries
and screams out in the scotch broom.

Beyond these more constant presences,
an occasional red fox footed softly
through the field and a pack of coyote
would gather around the little pond
on the other side of the blackberry thicket.
Their late night howls would wake me
from strange dreams of the animal world
forcing their way through the back door,
where I wrestled a moose and other creatures
that tried to cross the threshold into my world.
The rodents were the most persistent,
but I would win that struggle.

By the time I left the old white house
two deer had settled around five feet
from my bedroom window, and though
I never petted or fed them from my hand,
I would talk to them every day from less
than ten feet away as they would look up
from where they lay with such tender eyes
I knew they could feel our sweet connection.
I was sure I would miss all my animal friends
that populated the field in those overgrown years
but the deer most of all have visited me
out of the quiet moments into memory.

The End of the Story

After I moved out of the old
and faded white house
my children thought might collapse
upon itself like the lungs of the barns,
new America converged upon it.

Vagrants of the crashing economy,
meth-heads and scrounges came
to rifle through the remains.
They stripped the copper wiring
from the basement and scurried
up and down the stairs.

The cups and silverware, the old stereo
that did not work; they swept up
the useless along with the useful.

They slept in George's kingdom,
in Nana's magic house that smelled
like healing herbs and sage.
I doubt that they had made much
of what had happened here.
I found evidence of someone sleeping
beneath the big, imploded barn.
It was clear that the lost had come
like the deer and the raccoon to make
a home here at the end of the story.

My mother cursed several trucks away.
With "No Trespassing" signs posted,
they had no right on her property.
She even had to argue with a couple
of Native men who had just shot
one of the deer with an arrow.

They told her it was their right,
and the cop who came agreed
until she told them to get the hell
off her property before someone
accidentally shot at them.

I wondered if the unkempt field was a luxury.
My mother knew she was going to have to sell,
sell out the wildlife she had come to love,
sell out a lifetime of memories
because the taxes and liability
were a burden, and the encroachment
on the open space would not cease.

The Foundation

When I got back to Renton,
there was a big backhoe
taking bites of mangled wood
from the side of my Nana's house.
They were nothing less than
systematic butchers of our past.

My mother's face was flustered red.
Three times already up and down
the menacing road. When I arrived,
she said: "they are destroying my life."
She lived there as a child,
lived next door most of her years.
The field, the stomping grounds
for the Prince of Poverty Row
and his ponies, sold, soon to be plowed.

I swept her up from her despair
and drove her through a number of chores,
eventually stopping for lunch
at the Pot Belly, down at The Landing.
We ate sandwiches and sipped shakes.
Told a few stories and read that poem
by Bishop on "the art of losing."
She folded the copy twice
and put it in her purse.

When we returned to the site,
only the chimney stood proud.
Everything else a pile of rubble,
except for the foundation
which seemed exceptionally small.
Such a tiny footprint for such
a giant step. So many dreams inside,
so many stories, at least a hundred
levels high: the champion horses,
the baseballs whizzing through flight,
all of it already right now.

All of it right now I thought.

Later, Tara and her children came over.
Scott and Shannon called.
When Rick got home, we all
went back down there again together
and wandered the overgrown field.

Return of the Backhoe

The backhoe came today, prehistoric
in its gangly yellow metal jacket.
It rumbled into the first field
where the apple trees the deer
fleeced every year still flourished.

Its big bucket mouth ripped
through the black berries and scotch-broom
which had eclipsed the openness
where the horses grazed and we
as children invented games.

One big gash around the perimeter
was enough to disturb the balance of wildlife.
A rat scurried under the fence and into the ditch.
A family of raccoons single-filed their way
up toward the corner of the big field,
but there would be no place to hide.
I watched a six-point buck bound the fence
and move from yard to yard seeking cover.
My mother shivered in the heat of noon.

They would tear down her fence
and chop down her old rotting poplars.
She fretted over where the birds would go
who'd fed from her feeders
that hung in the low branches.

The mice too, she said, fed
from the overflow of spilled seed.
She had fed them all, raccoon, deer,
mice, rats, birds… and loved
the wildness that thrived around her.

Body and the Battlefield

When the field becomes the body,
wind floating through green branches,
deer attentive in the thick shadow

as a hawk swoops a mark
in the stubble and the hooves
of horses beat out the bass
from fence to fence on the drum,

we no longer stand apart.
The heart spreads through the opening
like daybreak over the eastern hills.
How can we explain the light
that lets us in or the eyes
we have learned to let out
like the wild heart from its cage?

I am the hawk. I am
the deer who came from here.

My mother and brother
who still live above the field
must feel the bulldozers
grumbling over and grinding under
the haven of the raccoon
and the tranquility of the deer.

What we've held so close
like a lover or a child
has become the battlefield.

Our attachments are torn like flesh
with their chainsaws in the big trees!

My Mother's Paces

Every day my mother paces up and down
the busy road calling out to workers
for some element of their plan
that she can no longer understand.
Each day they repeat their conversation,
"We will not cut down your trees and strip
your property until we have the sewer in place."
Each day in her disorientation she forgets.

We have to measure the distance
to the stakes on the south-side of her fence.
Fifteen more feet every time, but she forgets.
The facts just slip like grease into the past.

She paces the old gravel road aghast
at how little property is left out back.
"They took more than I wanted," she gasps
and haunts the neighbors' yards like a ghost
hovering close to their fences to see
painfully what no longer exists.
The land and the story both
seem to fall through her arms
like loose hay, like the horses
that galloped away into thin air.

They fall through her arms like her
mother and father whose impressions

had remained in the house, in the barn,
in the silhouette of the garden,
her dogs, cats, raccoons, deer, the swallow
that returned every year into thin air.

To have everything pulled out from under
you, the land you loved stripped bare,
the man you loved no longer here,
the animals you fed and gathered near
with no longer a place for them to thrive.
How does one stay alive staring into the face
of such absence, of such permanent loss?

We kneel beside her and join her prayers,
these prayers for all things great and small,
these prayers for the spirit to fill
the emptiness of living and dying here
with the pure transcendence of love,
these prayers that fall with the words below,
the spirit rising to sustain her above.

Familial Frames

The Black Box

My hands dip deep into the black box
pulling out topaz rubies pearls
of pictures clinking together
and murmuring the past
little echoes that grow the more
I delve into the shadows of before

A little ballerina and a stout man
bareback rodeo on horse and steer
my mother and her wild father
out front on his white palomino
winning the derby year after year

A family fresh from Italy
they look so old world as they
pose together with their dark
skin and old fashion attire

A great grandfather arms spread
wide for his family to follow
after crossing the cold Atlantic
disappearing state by state
as we track his name and travel

New York Alabama New Orleans
until arriving at the last frontier
the northwest of the new world

Hungry worn thin seeking
for the final place to put
his root and begin again

What could have driven him
to cast away in the hull of a ship
for weeks at sea waiting for the horn
to blow at the sight of land

Was it the drum of impending war
the future plight of hapless soldiers
or perhaps a government stealing
land and silencing the little man
as the cry and desire for freedom
summoned from somewhere afar

Writing his wife to join him
after two years a promising letter
Old world healer full of faith
coming forth through the unknown
to blossom into motherhood

Covered in coal dust black lung and
broken backs these men from before
some lost in the dynamite blasts
deep in tunnels of the mine shafts
forefathers who brought us here

Turning the page to recent years
the dandelion blown far and wide
grown into musicians and engineers
lawyers and poets spun from the soil
and the toil of blood into tomorrow

These portraits from the past
when they were still young seem
so full of hope for the years to come
We wear their features and carry
their blood and bear their dreams
and the burden to make good
their sacrifice and the fierce will
never to submit to a diminishment
of the pride and freedom we feel

Barnardo Odonin, my great grandfather on my Mother's side, left the outskirts of Turin, Italy in 1906 to find a new home in America and start a family with his wife Dominica, our Noni. His adventure took him through Ellis Island in New York, Alabama, New Orleans, and other unknown destinations, searching for work and the best place to create a viable foundation.

This is the family that Barnardo and Dominica created in the far corner of America, the state of Washington. Dominica joined her husband in Cle Elum, after his two-year trek, where their eldest child, our Nana, was born in 1911. From left to right, back row: Rosie, Mary, Noni, and Barnardo. Front row: Barbo and Kathleen, our Nana.

This is Grampa George and the Great Uncles on a hunting trip in Winthrop, Washington. This picture becomes a central image in the vignette, "At the Funeral of Chao Pegoraro." From left to right, back row: Pete Marconi, Chao Pegoraro, George Ouimet, Ernie Ouimet. Front row: Barbo Odonin.

George Ouimet came back from working in the fields in Canada and ultimately left his professional pursuit as a fighter to marry the magical Kathleen Odonin.

This is an early picture of Sally Ouimet, my mother, and her little brother, Richard Ouimet, Dick, who grew up to be an engineer and famously, to our family, worked on many of the Nasa space projects. They both grew up in the field and beyond with such an incredible connection to animals and nature.

These three women created the maternal magic throughout my youth and beyond. The picture of two women standing on the rocks is of my mother and Nana, her mother. The single photo on page 102 is of Noni, Nana's mother, who died before I was born but was always a spiritual presence in my imagination because of my mother's stories about her.

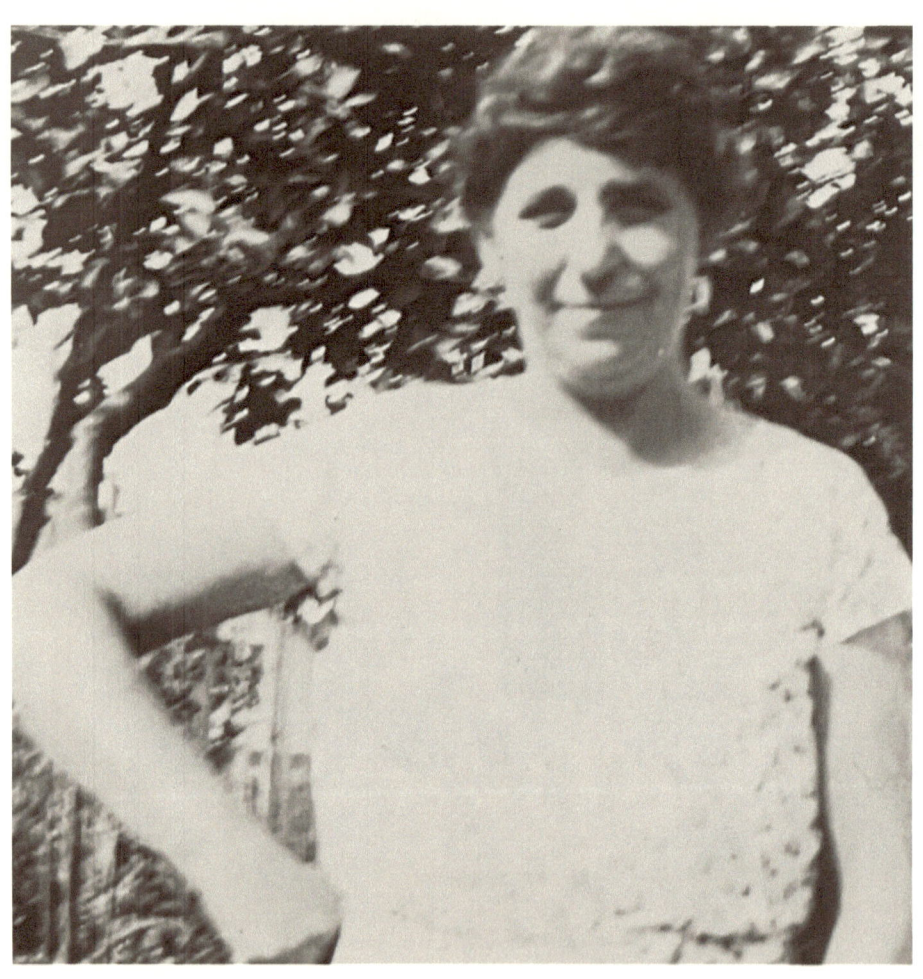

This is a picture of Noni, our Nana's mother, the one my mother said was the most beautiful person she ever knew.

This is Sally, my mom, and her favorite horse, Princess Littlebit. They won many ribbons and trophies together in various horse and rider competitions. She becomes part of my mother's daydream in "Past Present" in the "Maternal Magic" chapter.

In the early years, it was riding horseback and steer in a horse club and at rodeo competitions that brought my Father together with my Grampa, as well as with his daughter, my wild and beautiful Mother, who he almost instantly convinced to marry him. "She asked, do you love dogs?" He replied, "I love dogs!" "If he had said no," she would always say, "I wouldn't have married him."

My mother and father beaming with Joy at their wedding.

My brother Rick and I are sitting on a fence with cowboy hats and guns imagining a world of the wild west, the beginning of the many fantasies and games we envisioned and created in the field. Several poems in the "Further Afield" chapter develop this theme.

My brothers and I were part of the next generation to grow up within the dream of the field. We lived 384 feet away from Grandpa and Nana's house. This is a picture of the three of us on Nana's old couch where I would sleep when I spent the night as a child. From left to right: Rick, Pat, and me.

Uncle Dick and his wife Ann's four children also grew up spending a lot of time in the fabled field, especially when they were young. This picture takes place at one of the many birthday parties in my Mom and Dad's house, which he built on an upper corner of the field. From left to right: Kathy, Jeff, brother Pat, Karen, Me, brother Rick, and in front, at the head of the table, Kim. All are mentioned in the poem, "Family Picnics."

618 Longacres 9/6/64 ROSES SUCCESS   James Prouty-up
BIG MOMMY-2nd   George Ouimet-trainer
GAD ZOOKS-3rd   5 1/2 Fur 1:05:3 Mr & Mrs George Ouimet & Son-owner

In this picture I am the six year old standing in front of my Dad, while Uncle Dick and Grampa hold Roses Success for the photo. This is the first of many wins to come from the stable my Grampa bred and trained.

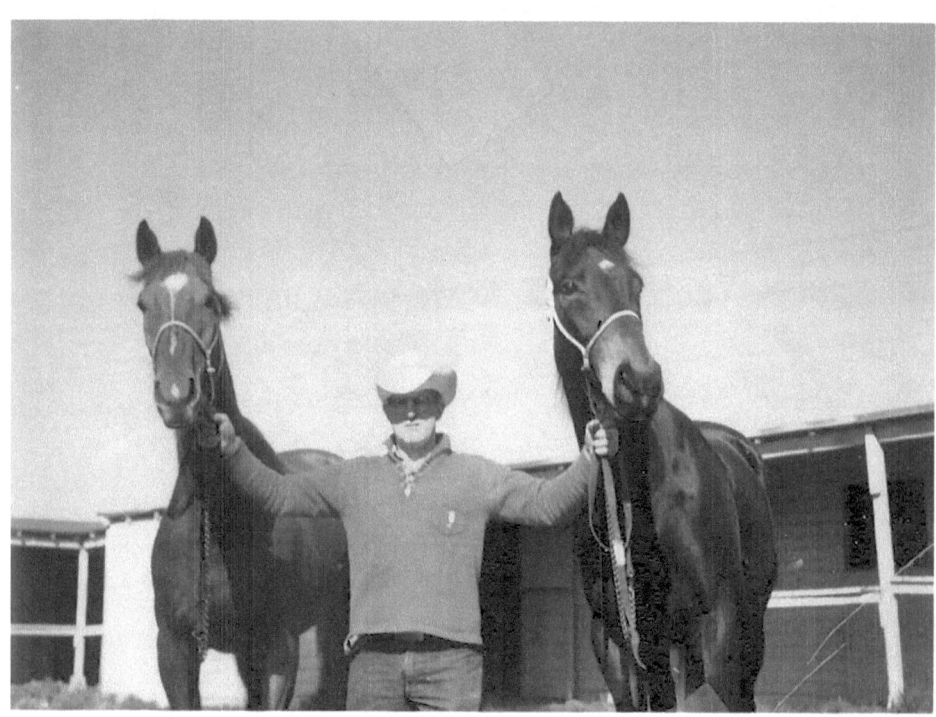

My Grampa holds his two favorite horses, No Friction, the hybrid saddle horse and racer, and He Did Alibhai, his great champion. It was an anomaly to get them so calmly close together; they had such a contentious competition across their whole lives.

Prince of 'Poverty Row'

BY JOE MOONEY

The inventory for George Quimet's operation at Longacres is inauspicious. But then, so is George. By choice, one suspects.

The address is "Poverty Row," the backstretch panhandle, squeezed into a narrow strip of ground left over between the track and a county road. (They say when you get down here, you're "on your way out.")

George has been there for years, again by choice, turning down a number of track offers to move him into more fashionable quarters. "I like it here," he insists. "It's more like being out in the country."

His list of assets includes four thoroughbreds, one of whom, He Did Alibhai, is no longer afflicted by homesickness; another of whom, No Friction, suffers from an identity crisis (he does not wet the bed, however) and two others who actually need very little psychoanalytical attention.

Though it's not generally held against them, the former two are products of $100 breedings. Their papa, Mr. Mustard, has since gained respectability, but one can easily appreciate the trauma of those early days.

In the case of No Friction, a large, nearly black, seven-year-old gelding, the problem is especially acute. George picked up his dam, Shota, for the mind-boggling sum of $50 back in 1953. This plainly was tourist class.

Small wonder No Friction was prey to a fast talker like George.

"I thought of putting him on a plow. Have him turn over some ground at the ranch," George says, surprisingly. His chin protrudes and his lips parrt in a typical grin—a joke. What is surprising is that he hasn't actually done it.

No Friction, when he isn't hauling George through the Cascades, hunting deer, does a convincing routine as a race horse, holding his own as a $4,000 claimer, only a modest drop from allowance ranks at Longacres. He also holds a part-time position as George's lead pony. (Part-time here means every morning.)

Now, this is not your classical conditioning agenda for a thoroughbred.

So unorthodox is it, in fact, that George has received — and turned down — an offer of $3,200 from a Californian interested in making No Friction a saddle horse, of all things.

No purist, George responded that $4,000 sounded more like it. The buyer's agent blanched. "For a saddle horse?" he asked in disbelief.

George smiled, taking keen pleasure in retelling the story. "A week later he won for $4,000." And George was still the owner.

GEORGE OUIMET AND HUNTING PARTNER

No Friction delivers in the woods and on the track

"Heck, a guy offered me a Cadillac for him," George continued. "Course, it was a two-year old Cadillac."

George recalls when the horse was foaled and he and his wife Katy (Kathleen) were trying to decide on a name for him. He was a huge colt. "You could push a bale of hay through his forelegs," George described.

Katy cracked, "There won't be any friction there."

Describing his hunting trip with the big gelding, George admitted No Friction had been nervous in the trailer, but had immediately settled down once outside.

Asked if he had to take special precautions securing the horse in the woods overnight, George said, "Naw. Just hung a hay bag on a tree and tied him up."

The horse was spared the indignity of having to pack a deer back to the edge of civilization. George was skunked.

George uses No Friction virtually every morning to squire stablemates around the track. "He trains this one," George says, nodding to He Did Alibhai. "I never put a boy on Alibhai."

Nevertheless, with a keen sense for irony, George insists on a lead pony for No Friction whenever the gelding goes to post

title of the article says it all. The Seattle *Post Intelligencer* wrote two articles in which they referred to our mpa as the "Prince of Poverty Row," because of his great success with his horses and his desire to remain ng the smaller stables and trainers on the back road of Longacres Racetrack.

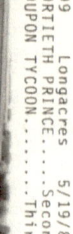

BARBARIC GEORGE

299	Longacres	5/19/84		M/M George Ouimet..Owner
FORTIETH PRINCE.......Second				George Ouimet....Trainer
COUPON TYCOON.......Third				Frank Brown.........up

EVERETT ELKS PURSE

6 fur.   1:10.1

Barbaric George was my Grampa's last big winner. This shot in the Winner's Circle was taken after one of his victories. A good gathering from my side of the family was in attendance. From left to right; Diane, my wife, me, Lois Neilson, Tony Milonas, Lori, Rick's wife, Rick, Kristy, Pat's wife, Pat, and Louie, my Grampa's best friend. This is one of the last photos of my Grampa George holding one of his horses in the winning circle. Barbaric George would continue to race with Louie, after he inherited him in George's will.

112

This is the field that the generation after ours came to know, one of deer, raccoon, coyote, and that last nasty little Shetland pony. From Rick's family both Shannon and Tara lived with Nana and benefitted from her wisdom in their high school years. T.J., his son, was also a frequent visitor when he was young. My three boys, Byron, Alex, and Scott spent a great deal of time with both my Nana and Mom and wandered the field often. Pat's children, John, Melissa, Tony, and Julia also spent many days and nights with my Nana and Mom and grew up around the animals that inhabited the field. My cousin's children as well would come to visit Nana and the world that Grampa George left behind. Kathy's boys, Michael and Nick Torretta, and Karen's children, Michele, Max, Alex, and Angela all carry forth some memory of the dream.

This is the big barn that collapsed around the time that people began to fleece the garage and house of everything useful or useless they could take. Only several years later the tractors and backhoes would come to tear every standing bush, tree, and structure down and completely remake the face of the land.

Half Horse Half Man

Wild and Free

Wild people love honor and loyalty because they know there is no true law, but the property and power of the will unto itself and the mystery of the spirit. I grew up in a field between the road and the wild woods. Without knowing I straddled the fence between two worlds. My Grampa was a primal man, a fighter, half horse, half man. The horses loved him, and the men feared him. The men loved him, and the horses feared him. My Nana came from the old world healers. Her house smelled like mint and sage or a kind of magic herb. When you sat at the table and chatted with her, the turbulence and confusion of clouds would clear. She would just smile, pour out a glass of milk, offer the cookies and deal the cards. I had no idea about how she was dealing out my future.

Out on the road as the years passed, the traffic got thicker and louder. It grew hard to think clearly. There were so many things you were supposed to do, but when I turned my back on that cacophonous confusion, I could hear the birds again with their medley from the bushes. I could see the field extended like a doorway into the mountains and the endless above.

There was a freedom we learned out here on the edge of society, a freedom to feel your way through a subtle connection with nature into the heart of what is wrong and right. Honor came from this natural dignity, the way Alibhai would bow his neck and strut the field, the same way he would strut in front of a roaring crowd after a win at the track, but more gently, yet just as proud. To live with pride by your own discrimination and will was a freedom that came by living within the suspension of the field.

He Did Alibhai

My Grampa had one great horse named He Did Alibhai, a beautiful chestnut who exceeded his name. When they were young, Ali, as we called him, and No Friction, who were born in the same year, would break down the fences to fight each other for alpha status of the field. Beyond their competition with each other, they both were kind and gentle horses. I don't think either one of them ever bit a person. Watching Ali run through the field, dazzled by his long strides and grace, my Grampa knew he was going to be a champion. Both of these horses, born no more than a month apart, measured well above 16 hands, but Ali's body was sleek and long, while Friction, as we called him, was built like a strong, oversized saddle horse.

When they hit the track at three, my Grampa made the biggest mistake of his life. He entered Ali in a lower claiming race with a big purse. Although Ali had won a couple of races and had done two recent black-letter workouts, George was certain he would not be claimed at that price. In that fateful race for a big purse, he broke from the gate ahead of everyone. Down the backstretch, you could see his long greyhound-like strides, distinct from the rest, pulling away by ten lengths. It was a mile race, and George wondered if he would have the stamina to hold on because he had never run this far before. Down the stretch, he was all heart and never looked back as he increased his lead by a couple more lengths and crossed the finish line all alone. The winning photo didn't even show the rest of the pack. My Grampa, who had always ponied his horses to the gate back then, handed his saddle horse over to another rider, and sprinted across the middle of the track to the winning circle on the other side. Ali bowed his neck, strutted, and snorted while looking up and responding to the roar of the crowd which he would become famous for across the years. My Grampa entered the winning circle with his chin out and a proud grin on his face, grabbing hold of Ali's halter as he whispered and chirped to his Champion. As the picture was being taken, (you can still see it on his face) they called out the names of the top three horses, the odds and the official time and then as if a plane had crashed through the side of his house, shattering the glory of his unfolding dream, he hardly heard the name of the man who had done it, but Ali had been claimed. George had tears in his eyes as he clutched his prize pony around the neck. His dream, his true champion, was gone.

The new owner immediately swept Ali down to the big tracks in California where the purses were bigger. We didn't hear much about Ali's success, but after about a full season, my Grampa, who had been living in perpetual remorse, heard that they had run him ragged and he had gone lame. That next season, Ali showed up at Longacres again and was eventually entered into a much lower claiming race. My Grampa decided to enter Friction in it as well, although it was a little above his grade. Friction had already won a race, but he was a longshot in this crowd.

My Grampa eyed Ali walking around the paddock with a limp and his head down. They had ruined him, he thought, a world class racehorse, and they had ruined him. He loved that horse so much. When he let out a couple chirps, Ali pricked up his ears, turned his head and whinnied back to George. He was going to give it his best. My Grampa smiled and parted because he had something he had to do. When the race started, Ali broke out of the gate and took the lead by several lengths. George could see through his binoculars that his stride was uneven, but he still held the lead down the backstretch and through the final turn, where he was overtaken by a big heavy hoofed bay thundering down the stretch. "God dammit," my Grampa said to himself. "That's Friction!" My Grampa had almost completely forgotten he was in the race. Ali had fought to keep pace with his old rival, but his strides had become dangerously uneven. The jockey pulled him up while he was still in second place, struggling to stay with that big ass bay. He eventually crossed the finish line in the back by himself with a slow lame-looking trot. He had shown so much heart; he did not want to give up.

No Friction won that race with the fastest time of his career. He strutted by the stands, snorting with pride, bending his neck to look into the eyes of his sibling rival. My Grampa stood in the winning circle with one hand patting Friction's neck while the other held on to his halter. He started to laugh when they called out the names of the top three horses, the odds and the official time, then held his breath as it came: He Did Alibhai has been claimed by George Ouimet. That was one of the greatest days of my Grampa's life, and he would not regret the money he had spent.

He immediately brought him home to the ranch, and it made Ali so happy to be out munching grass in the big field next to the house where my Grampa and Nanna could keep an eye on him. I used to go out and pet him every day. Although a little aloof, he seemed smarter than the rest of the horses and had a noble carriage even with his lame limp. My Grampa fed him oats and hay every day to bring him back to health again. He also painted his ankles each morning with that magical medicine that took away all the swelling and drew those ankles up tight. There had been irreparable damage though, and the vet thought he may never run again. It doesn't matter," my Grampa replied. "I'm taking care of this horse for the rest of his natural life," but in his heart he knew he had a true champion and still imagined the big races they were going to win together.

The next season and really the rest of Ali's racing life, my Grampa had to be careful with him, only running him about half as often as his other horses. When he ran though, there was a huge fan base that never missed a race. They loved watching that long stride go from gate to finish line in first place. Ali won 18 races, 18 seconds, and 11 thirds as he took home many big purses across the years. In a Washington State Championship, he tied the world record for a mile and a sixteenth, but unfortunately ended up in second place because Grey Papa, a nationally renowned horse from out of state, broke it. Alibhai never lost when the track conditions were slop because the water on the surface chilled his ankles, and he could run as God intended. When he retired at 13 on a win, he left Longacres with the longest racing career in the history of the track. He came back home and walked the fields with his head held proud until he died at 33, a very old age for a horse.

Men Today

Grampa, looking back from where
you are in the air rising like mist,
in the inverse of gravity here
where all that rises knows the fall
that a spirit makes into existence.

Here we struggle as before.
There is loss; there is failure,
though Nana and your daughter
have held our world together.

Some things have been unavoidable.
Nana died at 96, 23 years after you.
The land where you made your stake
and rode your horses against the wind
has been at last sold to developers.

Here we struggle as before:
Taxes, vagrants, collapsing barns,
the white house cracking like old bones;
something had to be done, so we sold.
Stripped of everything you could remember,
if memory holds a place in your world,
the land is a blank page of dirt
with no thought of what it may produce.

Of course, there was once thunder here,
a garden green and the races

"we winned" as you would say
dancing a jig up the stairs.
There was laughter and joking,
the horses were bucking and we
were winning the lottery game.
It all felt so important back then,
cleaning stalls and wheeling hay.

The way we are living now,
the sedentary work and lifestyle,
so soft compared to the stormy
struggle of men from your generation,
might, if you can still see a reason
to care at all, disgust you a little.

I see no reason for revolt yet,
where there is no whip or gun,
no cruelty savagely at hand;
except this loss of freedom – not
just the open space of the field –
but the will to reject your thoughts
delivered by an expert – to having your mind
ground like coffee beans into fine flakes,
steeped in hot water under pressure,
and served to you for your pleasure.

I think men like you would resist.

Colt 45

Raising a stud horse is harder than a gelding.
They strut more and challenge authority.
I remember Colt 45 on summer nights,
the drum roll of his hooves through my dreams.

I would wake to the lather of his relentless gallop
and snorts so loud the dogs would bark.

Grampa would pasture him alone in the upper field
because he would strike out at the older gildings,
but the fences were still just feeble boundaries
between him and the fertile fillies.

Grampa said after he busted several fences,
I don't know if it's worth the trouble to leave him this way.
Maybe I should just cut 'em and put him out of his misery.
We pleaded with him to let him be; we had never
raised a stud horse and known something so wild and free.

The Prince of Poverty Row

1. The Stable

My Grampa bred his mares and raised his own thoroughbreds. His ten-acre ranch was a kind of paradise if you loved horses. I remember being awakened before dawn one morning, when I was around seven, to traipse down through the field to look at the newly born colt they called No Friction. In the gauze light glow of a dim bulb, I watched his long spindly legs wobble beneath his mother's teets. He was No Friction. I would later be his first jockey, as my Grampa carefully walked him and then gypped him in circles with me on his back. Even later, I would saddle him up to pony other horses in our stable at Longacres Racetrack. Friction grew to a nearly 17 hand moose of a horse that was a fair racer but would have been an ace pulling a plow. No Friction, He Did Alibai, Konnie Kim, Hitter's Pride, etc. My Grampa's horses were home grown and raised with a firm and gentle hand. "You never let them dominate you," he often said, "and never show them fear." He also encouraged us to talk to them often and give them lots of love. They became like pets to us. I remember Connie Kim and Blondie Spin galloping across the field when I called out to them. They would literally fall asleep with all the weight of their big jaws on my shoulder as I gently pet their foreheads. My Grampa's high-strung thoroughbreds were, for the most part, although big and dangerous, some of the most wonderful friends ever. I would say he was a kind of horse whisperer, or maybe horse tamer would be more apt.

2. The Apprentice

There were no illusions; horses are a dangerous animal. You would have to be a knucklehead to stand or walk behind one of them, or let them walk with their sharp heavy hooves on your feet, yet I always continued to press against the boundary between us. I even one time slid off a low hanging plywood tree fort onto No Friction's back; he was always my favorite back then. He had come in under the tree to get out of the rain. Several of them had. I knew they would be there and had been plotting this for weeks. I patted his neck for a while before I slowly slid on his wet back. Startled a little, he trotted out from under the tree and made a little circle in the rain. Once he slowed down, I quickly slid to my feet elated.

It was not, however, all love and kindness out in the field or down at the track. I got the wind knocked out of me falling off the old saddle horse, Smokey, riding bareback at five years old, and I got nipped a couple of times by Sally Anne and that damn Connie Rose. They both could be a little temperamental.

My Grampa was clear on how to handle a rank horse. You never let them get the best of you. One time I came up to Sally Anne in the open field and grabbed hold of her halter to give her a pet, and she ripped her head back and tried to break free of me. Now, my Grampa always said, "you never let them go; don't let them think they can dominate you." So I held on tight as she reared straight up into the air. I tucked my body up under her belly as she struck out with her front hooves on either side of me. When she came back to the ground, I managed to kick my legs back onto my feet and push her away long enough to break into a sprint toward the fence. I could hear her right behind me as I took a superman leap over the five foot divide and got up on the other side unharmed. I rose to my feet exuberant with my success. I couldn't believe I actually pulled it off.

When I had bounced up the field and entered the house, I heard the phone ringing and picked it up. It was my Grampa; he had watched the whole incident from his window. "God damn it Mikey," he said. "I thought I told you never to let them go! Now she's gonna think she can dominate you."

I never fully understood what he wanted me to do out there, but over the years it became a little clearer the kind of man he wanted me to become.

3. The Horse Whisperer

As I tell the following stories, it is important to keep this in perspective. My Grampa treated his horses better than anyone I ever saw at the track. He petted them and groomed them often, gave them honey every morning and talked to them like his best friends. Around the track, he was famous for his ability to handle a rank horse. Bat, the old gate keeper for the races, would call him over the intercom to help teach a jumpy horse to settle down in the starting gate, or various trainers would call him to help load a recalcitrant horse into a trailer.

One time I watched a group of men struggle for nearly an hour trying to get a bucking and kicking bay thoroughbred in a trailer. Finally, I heard them say: "let's go get George," George Ouimet, the Prince of Poverty Row, as the papers called him because of his unusual success as a small stable trainer. The Seattle Post Intelligencer once featured a picture of him and No Friction, his part time saddle horse and thoroughbred racer, on the front page of the sports section.

My Grampa walked right up to that terrified, wall-eyed bay and took hold of the shank and gave it a sharp jerk to get the horse's attention. Before the horse knew what was happening my Grampa had stepped into him and was rubbing down his neck and talking to him with a soft chant. In less than a minute, he walked him peacefully into the trailer and said: "there you go boys." And this was him, the horse whisperer, but this wasn't all of him. He had also been a professional boxer and he took shit from no man or beast.

4. The Horse Tamer

At the racetrack, it was common for horses to lunge their heads out of the stall and try to take a chunk out of your shoulder. My Grampa's horses, for the most part, did not do this. He had raised them differently. Although he rarely claimed another man's horse, he one time got a steal on Zae Phanney Dee, a sixteen hand bay with good legs for running. I never liked this horse, at least not at first. He was mean; he would hurt you. One time he kicked the hat off my head when I pulled him off the electric walker in front of our shedrow. On another occasion, he lunged his head out of the stall and sunk his teeth in my brother's shoulder. This was all the beast my Grampa was gonna take. He told my brother to latch the wooden doors on the stall after he slipped beneath the netting. We heard the pounding of hooves through the walls and a heaving and a grunting as our Grampa fought that animal with uppercuts and kicks to the belly, using the dimensions of the stall as a kind of ring to work around him.

At one point he flew out the bottom door and slid on his butt in the shed row. We couldn't tell whether he had been kicked or just pushed out the unlatched door. "God damn it Ricky," he said. "I told you to lock both doors," and then he stepped right back in the ring to finish the bout of wills. After another couple of minutes, the crashing of hooves on the wall and the thuds of a foot and a fist subsided. Everything became completely still. We stood there anxiously leaning forward to hear, when he finally said: "Okay Ricky, you can open the doors. And there he was rubbing Zae Phanny Dee down his back and scratching his belly, and telling him that everything was gonna be just fine, and it was.

The Last Pony

The years that followed my Nana's death,
long after my Grampa had departed
and nature encroached unbridled
upon his absence in the field
I lived in their house that had become
like an Ark with so many animals near.

The deer slept five feet from my bedroom,
rodents climbed inside the walls
and an abundance of birds swarmed
and swooned with their song.

My sleep was often broken
by shrieking raccoon or coyote cries.
In my dreams I wrestled with that host
of animals squeezing through the back door,
as if they were trying to climb aboard
before the future flood upon the field.

The years of the horse that came before
were inextricable from my childhood:
gazing at new-born foals
in the lamp-lit dark,
breaking young thoroughbreds,
the first on their backs,
and the backbeat of hooves
through sultry summer nights.

The years of glory at the track,
the Prince, the Whisperer, George Ouimet;
He Did Alibhai, the fastest horse of the pack,
No Friction, Connie Kim, and Blondie Spin,
some of my best friends ever;

the smell of horsehair everywhere,
the power, grace, and speed,
I inhaled it all into my spirit
and wandered into the world beyond
with the horse in my heart.

After Alibhai died, after all
the great brood was gone,
Duke, the Shetland pony, who had been
bought for the great grandchildren
and haunted the lower overgrown field,
I heard had died; this little beast was
the last of our great primal stable.

A nasty little thing, so unlike
the noble brood my Grampa bred
and trained to show respect.
He bucked every kid off his back
and bit hard if he had the chance.

He even broke the other Great Gramma's arm
when she tried to ride the cute little thing.
I never liked him; he tried to bite
or kick me each time I was near.

When my mother asked my brother and me
to drag his dead body from the lower field
to where the glue people could find him,
I was stunned by the irony.

When Rick and I picked him up with a burlap sack,
he weighed like a cardboard cut-out of a horse.
As we carried him to the road, I thought
this is what has come of all that force Grampa
mastered with fire and blood in the field.

Mostly Bereft

The hollow bell tone deadens my ear
I look for flowers and sunshine
while walking through a noonday
funeral where my grandfather finds
the missing hole to his endless mind
He'll never return to tell his stories
to me upon a broken knee

I see six people all dressed in black
and sorrow melting like wax
from the sun like syrup on the trees
Who can see the lack
in those who cannot see

I sit on a broken chair
one leg missing on the corner
that teeters at the cliffs edge

There's no peace anywhere
when you're still
like a Mack truck in a traffic jam
like a coin that lands
at the bottom of a well
after the wish has gone to hell

Six people all dressed in black
My Grampa won't be coming back

Upon your storied knee I learned
that dreams can change reality
but as you fade like a shadow
to your grave – I grieve

The shade from these token trees
feels cool but there's a creek
that some cruel God has turned to brick
and six people all dressed in black

walking backwards through time
and your wild soul on horseback
seeking beyond that mystical track

My Grampa won't be coming back

Last Words

The Field Beyond

Love was waking up to the field.
The delirious hooves of that stud horse
raging through hot summer nights
yielded to mornings of the robin
and sparrow and the mellow light
in the buttercups and daisies,
the green expanse spread like jam on toast.
When I opened my eyes, I looked out
to a world unified by that connection inside.

The power of the horses with their lyrical strides,
the trees with their nicknames, the deer
that came to settle in their shade, the raccoon
in the scotch broom or beneath the junipers
nestled against the house, the coyote that
slaked their thirst in the little pond, the rare bob
of the red fox bounding through the high grass,
the deep dug well that hid a deeper
meaning at the bottom of its dark shaft.

Everything emerging from a wavering dream,
with love embracing a certainty that this
was the dwelling of the suspended space,
where all that was one was welcome,
where the animals returned,
where the ancestors came,
where my father would return long after

his death to whisper the secret
through a sudden wind or ember
of memory so we might not forget.
The soul, which can roll out away
from us into an indefinite orbit,
yearns to fuse with such a place
where the ground has been consecrated
with the sweat of affection
with the sunrise of the eyes
that might witness the wonder,
the gesture of a friend saying goodbye,
the face of the beloved at your side.

I've had love all my life,
the first love engendered and swept
through the tall grass and the trees,
in understanding that the animals
were equal to me, my favorite horses
come rumbling to my call, my neighborhood
friends who grew into the suspension,
the past, the present, and now the future
that I carry with me with this secret
rooted deep within, even though
the tractors and back-hoes have come
with their steely indifference and stripped
the land bare of the memory of the fusion,

the recipe of soul to spread and open
its angelic wings like sunshine nestled
in each corner of perception performing
the impossible act of redemption
even in the face of such extreme loss.

Love is the answer to all this painful division
that thrashes through the fences and tears
apart the garden and the sweetest intentions
of the lover and his passion, of the knower
and his wisdom toward everyone that enters
the expansion of the sacred field.

Dog Bones

My mother says we cannot sell
the remaining land; this is where
the bones of the dogs are buried!
Of all the animals, they were
the closest, the most loyal.

I can count 18 dogs in my 60 years.
All but one are bones in the ground,
and the horses too who have passed
through are all gone. So it is with the hawk,
and the deer and the raccoon; all that
is passing through will one day pass away.

Hallowed is the ground they walked upon.
Hallowed is the field; hallowed is the ground
wherever life has grown and blood has spilled,
wherever eyes have lit the vision of the field.

We bury what we love when it's gone;
I loved them all and consecrate them
beneath this grass that grows
from the memory of these poems.

Nana's Last Words

When Nana died, she left us
with this strength and pride.
Struggling in the hospital bed
for weeks with cancer in her chest
and the MRSA spread through her blood,

she could have easily succumbed
to the wincing hopelessness; instead,
each time we entered the room,
it was like when I was a child,
her charms and faith in us
were her only purpose.

The day before she died,
she sprang up from days of darkness
crawling across her delirious sleep
to tubes in her nose and bruised arms
and the hum of monitors in the room.
When she looked up, she could see
her family gathered around her bed.
With a spark in her eye and a lucid mind
she took a moment with each of us,
a soulful glance, an affirmation of love
and a faith in the fire that burned within.

She told me to tell Byron who was off wandering

through Italy that she knew he was with her,

and then she pleaded with me to get her back home

to her own bed and chair at the window.

She said, Mike, I know you're the one

that can make it happen; for the entire day,

I pressed the doctors and the rest of the family.

I really tried, but she left the next morning

for her home with George in the unknown.

At the Funeral of Chao Pegoraro

It was the same plot of ground at Mt. Olivet,
where Terry, Mary and Rosie had recently been buried.
My car knew where it needed to go.
I walked over a hundred gravestones
on my way up to the tent
they had pitched for the occasion.
When I arrived, the embraces felt weary
with the weight of loss across the last few years.

There were two posters of pictures
displayed on easels above the grave.
I remembered the stories of Chao,
a tough barnacle of a man
who made it to 96. They said,
"he never stopped working, wouldn't
take his breaks back in the coal mines."

I looked at Chao and his brother in baseball uniforms.
Someone said that Ermo played until he was 81.
They were younger in the picture with their hands
in their gloves. There were portraits of Carol, his daughter,
and Rosie, his wife, my mother's aunt, who was always
so brash with her opinions of the rest of us. I liked her in the end.
She too gone now like so many I found on the posters.

One picture in particular startled me:
Five men on a hunting trip in Winthrop, someone said.
Yes, one was Chao Pegoraro, another Barbo, my Nanna's
barrel chested brother, who was kind but grew belligerent on liquor,
then there was Pete Marconi, the man who married the other sister, Mary:
Uncle Pete who got caught making moonshine and paid the fine.

And finally, like iron, like rock, in the middle
of the group, with a chin that stuck out like a dare,
so sure life could be hunted down and conquered.
This was my Grampa, George Ouimet, Prince of Poverty Row.

Each of them so self-assured, at the peaks of their power, around 30,
I thought. I too, like them, knew everything once, like my children now,
that certainty of stubborn feet that will walk their own way no matter what.
Both these faces of the past and these footsteps into the future
left me standing there alone looking for more from myself
and reaching within for the passion and strength to prevail.

The Dream

After all the horses had run out their years
and my wild Grampa had been swallowed by cancer
and Steve, the Mad Captain of our youth, had fled from Never Never Land,
once the little kids had all grown up and forgotten what they once imagined
and the spotted deer who had made their home in the middle of the Little Trees
were driven off the property by the violence of bulldozers, back-hoes, and graters,
and the pack of raccoon that had fought for their place in the scotch-broom
fled to the upper corner and slipped under the fence and exited the dream
and the fox who had fetched the confidence to strut out in the open
was never again to be seen and the coyote who held their gatherings around
the shallow pond and howled their revelry through the night were gone for good
and the owl who made his rounds to perch on the same pole each dusk
and the hawks whose homes in the fir trees were cut to the ground never again
to be found stalking the stealth of snakes and rodents in the high grass
and my mother who had long established her sanctuary for the song birds
and all the other animals that crossed into her world was fraught with concern
and my Nana with all her wisdom in her 96th year parted from this earth
and my father with all his intelligence and kindness was struck early by a stroke
and tumor and left it to us, his three boys, to remember the unspoken spirit
and the vagrants who had come to squat in what remained of the collapsing barns
and the scavengers who had pilfered the stereo and silverware
and the meth-heads who had stripped the house of all its copper wire
and others who had pried the new padlock open and made the house
their shelter and crept the field after dusk and before dawn
and the two Native men who had come to hunt the deer with bow and arrow,
all of them swept up into a dark where memory begins to sputter and fail.

After the City of Renton had incorporated the field within the city limits
and raised the taxes — my mother and uncle had to sell — sell the dream
of our families building homes there in the future, the grandchildren
and the great grandchildren tethered together to that deep love and unity
of blood with the soul that lives above in the suspended space of the field.

Between the Fences

The Field is long gone now.
I had wished my ashes to be
spilled in the high grass
with the buttercups and daisies,
scattered in the dark furze
of my Nana's gourded garden.

Our memories of late night
hooves on the drums of our dreams,
the neighing and snorts
of the lathered horses,
the Peter Pan games we played
with our close circle of friends.

The big tree and flats
apple, plum, and cherry,
bushes of juicy black berry
and the forts and hiding places
in the thick green cluster
of the little trees.

Today the steps we take
on the cement sidewalks
around the upscale houses
to places that no longer exist
walk further away from
the fading memories.

My children will carry
some overgrown image
of the dissolution of the dream,
the dilapidated and collapsing barns,
the fences with their crooked teeth,

our hikes through the crusted snow,
the soothing smells and healing
spells of Nana's house
like the magic of a fairy tale.

After the sun finally sets
and drains of all its color
and the wind forgets
the horses and the trees,
maybe only these words
will keep all that vitality between
the fences of living memory.

Keep Dreaming

Keep Dreaming

I keep dreaming about returning
to Nana's old white house
at the other end of the field
with her at the window
I'm still a child

I keep dreaming about returning
to my Mother's house
and she's still there
and the black labs
have not been buried yet

When I wake I dream
of going back in time
Not to fix things but rather
to bathe in the luminous light
and the nights as quiet
as a mumbled prayer

All the noise is not back there
the body bounding free
through the endless woods
with the dogs like a deer

When I go back there
I can see the horses rumbling
on the drum of the field

My Grampa is hefting bales
of hay through the air
and those childhood friends
are still there dreaming up
adventures without a care

I love going back there
to those breathless spellbinding days
They remind me to keep imagining
the future up in front of me
unfolding with magic through the haze

Blood Potion

There are some legacies that must be written down
to pass on as possibility to our children's children
so that they know the secret powers
possessed in this potion of blood and spirit

I remember how my mother's eyes shimmered
when she would tell me of Noni her grandmother
who she said was the most beautiful person in the world

She showed me God she said not in the Bible not
in a bevy of words but in the way she looked at you
in the clusters of birds that would pour into her
trees every year nesting in her sanctuary

Noni would bring a passion and a peace
into the chair where you sat into the air you
would breathe into the candles and tabletops
Anything could contribute to the strange
and true language she spoke to you

I never met her — she died before I was born
but I knew I could see her in the way my Mother
drew animals to her — sparrows every year nesting
beneath the deck and the raccoons she fed that slept
beneath the junipers against the front of her house

and I know I saw her through my Nana's wise eyes
watching my spirit carefully like an owl from the trees
with that invisible gift she shared with me over cards
cookies and milk when I was young and crazy with the bees

Together they have taught me the ruby magic
of my blood and the mystery of the spirit rising
I remember there are the stories that go further back
to Noni's mother in Turin a woman with the olive skin
of Calabria who people would come to see from villages
miles away to be delivered from the dark and their infirmity
I have no specific knowledge how she did this other than
the traces left in Noni my Nana and my Mother and me

Seeing the Field

The field stretches as far as the eyes
can squeeze the distance into sight,
as far as imagination can stretch beyond
the sense of what you can expect.

I carry the field wherever I go
like a book of dreams half written,
half yet to be seen unfolding
into constellations of flowers lit torch
bright in the night sky meadows of mind,
rolling with wheat waves like the sea,
tolling us back through each minute detail
to the quantum waltz of the infinite.

The field knows being only as the knower
knows what he is seeing is half true,
half the dream of his own ecstatic making.

Oh, the field of my youth was a blessing
and the horses that thundered athletic
into the dark with unshod hooves
pulse with each beat of my heart,
as it opens up to the act to making it new,
to a poetry of perception and the
permanent blue bled from the fire
to turn the deep dark into living light.

Play Ball

Between the fences I remember
the best friends in the world.
Some have died; the rest have gone.
They all seem so inaccessible.

We created ourselves in the open
spaces or high in the trees.
We made new words and phrases;
invention sprouted from our games.

As if some centrifugal force
plucked us from our proverbial tree,
every time someone moved it felt
like they fell out of existence.

Each year across the years,
we have gathered fewer and fewer
to play a summer and winter
game of baseball together.
At Carco, a local park, or Safeco,
a major league stadium; it didn't matter.

We have tried to recreate the space
where childhood yielded so much.
The field is where we return
not just to hear the echoes
of when we were inseparable

but also to imagine that
fluid freedom of boundless play,
the felt connection of the sunlight
flickering dizzy through the trees,
the whispering of soft feet in the leaves,
and the young girls in the high grass singing.

Once Again

The warmth of yellow in the tall grass
of the old field — which was once young
with thundering hooves and children
in the trees with no eye on the future
lost in the pure play of the arbitrary games
they made understanding without thinking
that it was nothing and everything just the same —
thaws the white frost slowly into strands of pearl
around a neck of shadow until the sluggish cold
of remembering what had been lost to that time —
which is clearly over once there is the thought
but never completely disappears into the golden
bowl of day — pulses into possibility again
and sweet return in the blackberry pluck
of the bounding boys and the lathered
horses — where there is everything that ever
was once and once only and once again

A Golden Gift

My gut churns like I'm in love,
but there is no object to my desire.
The fire that burns in me,
pistil and stamen, azalea and rose,
is a conflagration of flower.

The sap that rises through
bright green fingertips
on the branches of fir trees
bursts from my own on the page
and begins to form a living thing.

Love is what rises and makes
its offering on the altar of being.
It brings itself forth with
unbridled and fervent feeling
like horses with long fiery
manes feathered in the wind
galloping an open plain.

Wings of dove sail into seeing.
I can feel the lungs of life
breathe resuscitation into the
inert body of dirt and stone.

We were meant to come
thus in our eternal return
with love basking and burning
in the untamed golden flame.

The Last Acre

After the land had been sold, all but less than an acre, where my mother dug in and held out as long as her memories would keep her, the dream of the field became a story we would tell, like some might talk of Never Never Land or Paradise. When memories grow into stories that gestate into writing, something more than dissolution abides. Riding on the winds of imagination, like the hawk crying out from above, these words are a prayer to all that has passed away and an incantation to all we wish to remain.

Toward the end, my mother uttered and repeated only a few phrases each time I visited. She would say, "When my husband asked me to marry him, I asked, 'do you love dogs? If he had said no, I wouldn't have married him." "Do you love dogs?" she asked, so many times, so sweetly, so humorously often, we had it engraved on her tombstone.

The dogs, the horses, the birds, the deer, and every other animal and spirit that came near to her were God's children as much as us and those who came before and those who would come after, as much as her, part of an endless caravan in a divine dream marching toward his presence. The field for her was a place where they rested, a sanctuary of grace and blessings. She fed them all from the apple trees and feeders, the plates she placed out on her porch and yard, the buckets of water to keep them from crossing the dangerous road.

Her sanctuary had been reduced to less than an acre. We tried to keep the little field mown with a John Deer tractor, but she refused to cut down the wildflowers, and when the scotch broom bloomed and proliferated, she would not let me pull them out with a weed wrench, until pretty soon her little field was a jungle. I worked for a few years to keep her yard groomed and kempt, but she put up so much opposition to each bush I trimmed, each little tree or weed I pulled that eventually the jungle spread to envelop the house, as if nature would reclaim it as well. I knew she would be gone to earth before too long and that her soul would rise to that sanctuary beyond, that field where grace and the blessings come.

Bills and deeds got mixed with the trash. She no longer prepared her food to eat and could no longer remember when she last took her pills or had a bath. My brother Rick, her eldest son, lived with her and did everything he could to keep her healthy and hold her world together, as he had with our Dad, Grampa, and Nana, but the chaos spread wider and wider until one day she fell into that deep well in the overgrown unknown never to return.

We prepared to sell the house and land and watch the last slice of paradise bulldozed under and turned into three or four more luxury homes. Pat, her youngest son who lived close and had also done so much for her and our father through the struggling years, said: "Let's fix up that house; Dad built that house." In the days since, we have wrestled with that disheveled past, sorting through papers, taking out the trash, cutting down trees and unweaving the woven jungle. I have often thought about the wildlife that had still remained and was forced to slowly slip from what became the last blank page to plant and rewrite the story of this land. Where did they go? Did they make it to a new haven to live out their days. We did it for my father and mother; I'm proud that the house still stands, new roof and paint, some interior refinements, but it is still the place my father built and where we grew up together, a monument to what the new owners would never understand. I will always remember it as the place where we became the land.

www.ingramcontent.com/pod-product-compliance
Lightning Source LLC
Chambersburg PA
CBHW021155130626
46554CB00005B/1824